ESSENTIAL WRITING

1

From Sentence to Paragraph

Jethro Kenney

KINSEIDO

Kinseido Publishing Co., Ltd.
3-21 Kanda Jimbo-cho, Chiyoda-ku,
Tokyo 101-0051, Japan

First published 2023 by Kinseido Publishing Co., Ltd.

Design   Nampoosha Co., Ltd.

Overview

In *Essential Writing 1*, students take a step-by-step approach to develop skills and knowledge in basic sentence and paragraph writing. Each unit provides instruction on the essential structural and mechanical elements for producing good writing while actively engaging students in the learning process.

Essential Writing 1 is especially suited for beginner to low-intermediate Japanese English as a Foreign Language (EFL) students at the university level, but may be used by any level writer wishing to develop basic sentence and paragraph writing skills. Depending on the structure of classes at each university, the 12 units in *Essential Writing 1* can be taught over a 28-30-week academic school year by teaching one unit over a two-week period: thus, covering Units 1-6 in the spring semester and Units 7-12 in the fall semester.

Some of the highlights found in *Essential Writing 1* include:

◇ Opportunities for Active Learning

A majority of the over 75 exercises found in the book incorporate some element of pair work, making each exercise an opportunity to collaborate and actively engage students in the learning process.

◇ Model Paragraphs

Throughout the book there are numerous "model paragraphs" tailored to the beginning writer that provide students with examples of the structure and mechanics of quality writing. Additionally, the model paragraphs provide context for the target lessons found in each unit.

◇ Specific Areas of Focus

Each unit centers around a particular language focus that provides the learning target for that unit. These "Focus on" sections serve to help learners build the knowledge and skills needed to effectively produce a piece of quality writing.

◇ Common Errors

Many of the units highlight common errors made by beginning Japanese writers to address writing problems before they take place. This unique feature of *Essential Writing 1* will raise learner awareness and develop more independent writers.

◈ Vocabulary Checklists

The vocabulary checklists in *Essential Writing 1* are designed to develop a shared classroom language between the teacher and students. This allows for greater ease of communication when offering corrections and feedback. Additionally, these checklists facilitate increased responsibility and autonomy in the learner by ensuring that the student has understood the contents of each unit.

◈ Writing Checklists

Writing checklists found throughout *Essential Writing 1* serve as a quick reference for students to make certain they are meeting the demands of the assignment. These checklists are an invaluable resource for reinforcing the lessons found throughout the book to help students build good habits in formatting quality drafts.

Organization

Essential Writing 1 is made up of three distinct sections. "Part I: From Sentence to Paragraph" introduces the elements of sentence and paragraph structure and mechanics. "Extra: On Writing" introduces the approaches of product and process writing and provides a blueprint for properly formatting a written document. "Part II: Rhetorical Patterns," provides instruction, exercises, and assignments working with four different paragraph types.

PART I FROM SENTENCE TO PARAGRAPH

Part I is covered in Units 1-4. Units 1 and 2 provide a step-by-step approach to developing practical knowledge and skills, specifically, building basic sentences, avoiding common fragment errors, and building compound sentences for better writing clarity and fluency.

Units 3 and 4 focus on building paragraphs through practical knowledge and skills, including writing effective topic sentences, major and minor supporting details and concluding sentences.

EXTRA ON WRITING

"Extra: On Writing" is an intermediary between Parts I and II of *Essential Writing 1* that provides context and instruction on writing approach and formatting. Students often focus too heavily on producing the final work of an assignment, while missing the opportunity to engage in the writing process. "Extra" is a way of raising students' awareness that, while the final product is important, the process by which that final product is created is what develops the skills and experience needed for quality writing. Therefore, these two approaches are juxtaposed so that students can differentiate and gain greater control and understanding of both.

PART II RHETORICAL PATTERNS

Part II consists of Units 5-12 and provides instruction and practice using four different paragraph types: process, descriptive, narrative, and opinion. Each rhetorical pattern is covered over two units, giving students ample time to engage in the writing process before creating their final work. The exercises and assignments in these units reinforce the skills of sentence and paragraph building learned in Part I, while providing further instruction on the structural and grammatical characteristics of each specific paragraph type. Part II helps build confidence and paragraph writing experience through interactive exercises and assignments that engage learner interest.

APPENDICES

There is a brief set of appendices at the end of the book to offer some supplementary materials for select units. These resources can be used as part of the unit exercises or as additional reference materials at any stage of the writing process.

We hope that skills and practice covered in *Essential Writing 1* will prove a valuable and engaging resource in developing sentence and paragraph writing skills for university EFL students in Japan.

Jethro Kenney

ESSENTIAL WRITING 1

From Sentence to Paragraph

Table of Contents

Table of Contents

PART I

FROM SENTENCE TO PARAGRAPH

BUILDING THE SENTENCE

"You can make anything by writing." —C.S. Lewis

Sentences are the building blocks to paragraphs. To write well, we must know how to write **complete sentences**. A complete sentence, also called an **independent clause**, is a set of words that includes both a subject and a verb. It is also a complete idea that needs no more information to be understood.

An **incomplete sentence**, on the other hand, has either no subject or no verb, or it is a **dependent clause**. This means that it is an incomplete idea that needs more information to be understood. Incomplete sentences are also called **fragments**. In this unit, you will learn about four common fragment errors that new writers make.

COMPLETE SENTENCES

Focus on GRAMMAR Independent Clauses

A **clause** is a set of words that includes a subject and a verb.

As mentioned above, an **independent clause** has at least one subject and one verb, and its meaning can stand alone.

> Tomorrow is Wednesday.

> I see Mt. Fuji.

In each example above, a single subject and a single verb express a complete idea. These are **complete sentences**.

Circle the subject and underline the verb in each sentence below. Then compare your answers with a partner.

1. (The man) sat.

2. Yuji loves animals.

3. I received your email yesterday.

4. The woman sitting next to the window is my friend.

FRAGMENTS

Focus on GRAMMAR Common Fragment Errors

A **fragment** is not a sentence because it is not a complete idea. It may be missing a subject or verb, or it may be a dependent clause that needs more information to make sense. There are three common fragment errors that new writers make: 1) **-ing fragments**, 2) **infinitive fragments**, and 3) **dependent clause fragments**. A fourth sentence error, which we will call an 4) **example fragment**, is another common problem found in beginning writing.

1. The man **sitting** next to the window. (No verb.)

2. **To call** a good friend. (No subject.)

3. **When** the phone rang.
   (Has subject and verb but needs more information.)

4. **For example**, Saturday and Sunday.
   (No verb and needs more information.)

Discuss with a partner why the fragments above need more information to be understood.

EXERCISE 1 Identify Complete Sentences and Fragments

Work alone. Read the short paragraph. Underline the complete sentences and circle the fragments. Check your answers with a partner.

When I came home, the TV was on. My friend Hiro was there. Watching a movie. I have known him for six years. Since I was 14 years old. We met in junior high school. He loves animals. For example, dogs. To have as a pet.

EXERCISE 2 Identify and Correct Fragments

Read the following fragments. Work with a partner to make them into complete sentences. Don't forget punctuation, such as periods (.) and commas (,).

1. A brown dog.

   I can see a brown dog.
   _____

2. To buy a new car.

   _____

3. Raining tomorrow.

   _____

4. Because she doesn't like horror movies.

   _____

5. For example, pizza, hamburgers and ice cream.

   _____

EXERCISE 3 Read the Model Paragraph

Work with a partner. Read the short paragraph aloud one time each. Then work alone. Circle the subject and underline the verb in each sentence. Subjects may appear more than once, and sentences may have more than one verb. Then discuss your answers with your partner.

Last weekend I went to the park with my friend. We sat in the park and talked about our plans for the future. My friend said that he wants to travel in the future. He said he wants to see many places around the world. Most of all, he said he wants to visit Egypt. He is very interested in the pyramids and ancient Egypt.

EXERCISE **4** Write a Short Paragraph

Work alone. What did you do last weekend? Write 5-7 sentences describing what you did. Then circle the subject and underline the verb in each sentence.

Last weekend, (I) _____

EXERCISE **5** Listen for Detail

Work with a partner. You will take turns reading aloud your short paragraphs from Exercise 4. After your partner has finished reading, fill in the chart about your partner. If you do not know the answer, ask your partner.

What did your partner do?

Where was he/she?

Who was there?

CAPITALIZATION AND PUNCTUATION

Focus on GRAMMAR Completing the Sentence

Capitalization and **punctuation** are vital to writing complete sentences. Here are some rules for capitalization and punctuation.

- The first letter in a sentence is **capitalized**.

    She bought a new car.

- The first letter of a **proper name** is **capitalized**.

    Yesterday, **M**iki bought a new **T**oyota in **Y**okohama.

- Complete sentences usually end with a **period**.

    It is going to rain tomorrow.

- Questions end with a **question mark**.

    Is it going to rain tomorrow**?**

- Use an **exclamation point** to add emphasis.

    It rained every day for a month**!**

For more practice with capitalization, go to Appendix Unit 1. (➡ Page 100)

EXERCISE 6 Capitalize and Punctuate the Sentences Below

Work alone. Correct the sentences below with capitalization and punctuation. Then check your answers with a partner.

1. we left the hotel early in the morning

   We left the hotel early in the morning.

2. yuna wants to go to france more than germany

_____

3. are you sure he is from canada

_____

4. when is david going to arrive

_____

5. there is a spider in your hair

_____

EXERCISE 7 Let's Write

This is a short writing assignment to give you practice with the skills you learned in this unit.

For each of the questions below, write six or more sentences. Use the checklist to be sure you are writing correctly.

    1. Who are you? Introduce yourself.
    2. Where are you from? Write about your city, town, or country.

✓ Checklist

- ☐ Each sentence has a subject and a verb.
- ☐ Each sentence can stand alone. It is an independent clause.
- ☐ I capitalized the first letter of each sentence.
- ☐ I capitalized proper names of people, places and companies.
- ☐ I have punctuation at the end of each sentence.

✓ Vocabulary   Check the words you know, and review the words you do not.

☐ Clause	☐ Capitalization
☐ Independent clause	☐ Punctuation
☐ Dependent clause	☐ Proper name
☐ Complete sentence	☐ Period
☐ Fragment	☐ Question mark
	☐ Exclamation point

COMBINING SENTENCES

"One day I will find the right words, and they will be simple." —Jack Kerouac

A **simple sentence** is a single independent clause with a subject and a verb. Simple sentences are complete ideas that can stand alone. A **compound sentence** is two or more simple sentences often joined together by a comma and a coordinating conjunction. Writing with these two sentence types will improve writing fluency and communication.

SIMPLE AND COMPOUND SENTENCES

Focus on GRAMMAR Using Conjunctions for Compound Sentences

A **simple sentence** is a single independent clause with a subject and a verb.

> I love music.
> Andy has two black dogs.

A **compound sentence** is made of two or more independent clauses usually separated by a **comma** and a **conjunction**. Because an independent clause has a subject and a verb, there must be a subject and a verb on each side of the comma and conjunction.

While there are many conjunctions that serve different purposes, let's first focus on **contrast**, **similarity**, **result**, and **reason**.

- **But** expresses contrast.

> I listen to music, **but** I cannot play an instrument.

- **And** expresses similarity.

> Hitomi has two brothers, **and** they both live in Switzerland.

- **So** expresses a result.

> It is going to rain tomorrow, **so** the game is canceled.

• **Because** expresses a reason. (No comma.)

The game is canceled tomorrow **because** it is going to rain.

For more practice with conjunctions, go to Appendix Unit 2. → Page 101

EXERCISE 1 Correct and Write Compound Sentences

Work with a partner. Read the sentences below. They are all missing commas, and they are incomplete. Fix the errors and complete the sentences.

1. I have lived in Los Angeles but

    I have lived in Los Angeles, but I have never lived in Tokyo.

2. Every Tuesday they have a meeting so

_____

3. The report is due tomorrow but

_____

4. She does not have any brothers or sisters and

_____

5. We missed our flight back so

_____

6. I left the windows open and

_____

EXERCISE 2 Read and Correct Compound Sentences

Work alone. Read the short paragraph. There are five compound sentence errors. Find the errors and correct them by adding a comma. Next, circle the subject(s) and underline the verb(s) in each of the clauses. Finally, check your answers with a partner.

Kim is from Seoul, South Korea. He has lived in Japan for about six months and he really likes it. Kim still cannot read Japanese so I think it is hard for him sometimes. He recently started taking Japanese lessons and he is really improving a lot. He wants to go to a university in Japan but he will need to improve his reading ability first. I know he can do it. He is very hard working and he always has a positive attitude.

EXERCISE 3 Use Correct Conjunctions for Compound Sentences

Work alone. Complete the sentences below. Write *but*, *and*, or *so* on the line. Then work with a partner. Explain why you made your selections.

1. a. We always go to the same café on Tuesday _____ today it is closed.

   b. We always go to the same café on Tuesday _____ please join us.

2. a. I overslept _____ I missed my flight.

   b. I overslept _____ I did not miss my flight.

3. a. It is Nancy's birthday tomorrow _____ I have not bought her a present yet.

   b. It is Nancy's birthday tomorrow _____ I bought her a present.

SENTENCE PROBLEMS

Focus on FLUENCY Avoiding Choppy Sentences

To improve writing fluency, it is a good idea to use combinations of simple and compound sentences. This will make writing sound more natural and less choppy.

Simple sentences make more of an impact when you are writing. For example, in the following short paragraph the final sentence has a stronger impact than the longer **compound sentence**. This is because the reader only focuses on one point in the last sentence.

> Of all the places that I want to visit in the world, I think Peru is probably the most fascinating for me because I like Peruvian food, and I am interested in Machu Picchu. Machu Picchu looks amazing.

However, writing with too many simple sentences makes the writing choppy. **Choppy sentences** can sound too simple and robotic. For example, read the following:

> I want to visit Peru. It looks interesting. I like Peruvian food. I am also interested in Machu Picchu. It looks amazing.

Choppy sentences can be easily fixed by making a **compound sentence**. To make a compound sentence you must consider whether the two simple sentences are closely related, equal, or dependent upon one another. For example,

> I want to go to Peru. I will go next year.
> → I want to go to Peru**, so** I will go next year.

> I will visit Peru. I cannot speak Spanish.
> → I will visit Peru**, but** I cannot speak Spanish.

As you can see, these simple sentences are closely related. Therefore, they can be combined to form compound sentences.

EXERCISE 4   Edit the Choppy Sentences

Work with a partner. Read the short paragraph. Discuss which sentences could be made into compound sentences. Decide on which conjunctions should be used.

I have always wanted to go to Tanzania. I want to climb Mount Kilimanjaro. I want to see the animals. I am also interested in other countries in Africa. Tanzania is the most interesting to me. My friend is also interested in traveling there. We will try to go next year. We are excited about the trip. We have a lot to prepare before we go.

EXERCISE 5   Rewrite with Compound Sentences

Work alone. Rewrite the above paragraph with compound sentences. Then check your answers with the class.

EXERCISE 6 Let's Write

This is a short writing assignment to give you practice with the skills you learned in this unit.

Write a short paragraph to answer each of the two questions below. Use the checklist to be sure you are writing correctly.

1. Where is somewhere that you want to go. Why? Give details.
2. If you travel, who do you want to travel with? Why? Give details.

✓ Checklist

☐ Each sentence has a subject and a verb.

☐ Each sentence can stand alone. It is an independent clause.

☐ I capitalized the first letter of each sentence.

☐ I capitalized proper names of people, places and companies.

☐ I have punctuation at the end of each sentence.

☐ I have both simple sentences and compound sentences.

☐ Each compound sentence has a comma and a conjunction.

☐ I made compound sentences out of my choppy sentences.

✓ Vocabulary Check the words you know, and review the words you do not.

☐ Simple sentence   ☐ Capitalization (review)

☐ Compound sentence   ☐ Punctuation (review)

☐ Conjunction   ☐ Proper name (review)

☐ Comma   ☐ Period (review)

☐ Choppy sentence   ☐ Question mark (review)

☐ Fragment (review)   ☐ Exclamation point (review)

BUILDING THE PARAGRAPH

"Learn the rules like a pro, so you can break them like an artist."
—Pablo Picasso

The **paragraph** is the most basic unit of academic writing. A paragraph is where sentences come together on a single topic to form a complete idea, express an opinion, and convince the reader to agree with the writer's point of view. There are three parts to a paragraph: the **topic sentence**, the **supporting sentences** (or the body), and the **concluding sentence**. In this unit we will focus on the **topic sentence** and the **concluding sentence** because these two sentences serve a related function of binding the paragraph in a single topic.

Topic sentence	**This is the topic.**
Supporting sentences (Body)	These are the details.
Concluding sentence	**This was the topic.**

THE TOPIC SENTENCE

Focus on STRUCTURE Parts of a Topic Sentence

The topic sentence is usually the first or second sentence in the paragraph, and the most important sentence because it is what your paragraph is about. The topic sentence is made up of two parts: a **topic** and a **controlling idea**. The **topic** is the subject of the topic sentence and the topic of your paragraph. For example, if your topic is *music*, you can simply say you are writing about music. But what are you going to write about music? What do you want to say?

The **controlling** (main or central) **idea** is what you will say about the topic. It expresses a particular idea, opinion or point of view that shapes the type of paragraph you will write. For example, you may want to write a paragraph on how to learn music (a process paragraph).

Music **is easy to learn if you follow these three steps**.

Or describe the differences between various music genres (a descriptive paragraph).

There **are a few key differences between jazz, rock, and hip hop.**

Or maybe you are interested in describing how important music has been to you in your life (a narrative paragraph).

Music **is very important to me**.

Or maybe you want to write an opinion about how music impacts people's lives (an opinion paragraph).

Music **changes people's live**s.

In all of these cases, the **controlling idea** helps to shape your paragraph to express what you want to say about your chosen **topic**.

FEATURES OF THE TOPIC SENTENCE

Focus on STRUCTURE Characteristics of a "Good" Topic Sentence

Writing a good **topic sentence** is very important in paragraph writing. Let's look at some features of good **topic sentences**.

The **topic sentence** should:

Express an opinion or intention	Not just a simple fact
✓ Good	✕ Bad
Orcas are amazing hunters. There are three types of orcas.	Orcas are mammals.

Be a statement	Not a question
✓ Good	✕ Bad
Orcas eat a variety of other animals.	What do orcas eat?

Express a position	Not an announcement
✓ Good	✕ Bad
Orcas are the most dominant predators in the ocean.	This paragraph is about orcas.

23

EXERCISE **1** Identify "Good" Topic Sentences

Work with a partner. Identify and discuss what is "good" about these topic sentences. Are they *statements*? Do they *express an opinion, intention, or position*?

1. Last winter I had an amazing adventure.   (   )

2. It is easy to identify ripe avocados.   (   )

3. I have three big dreams for my future.   (   )

4. Living in a big city is stressful.   (   )

EXERCISE **2** Identify and Correct "Bad" Topic Sentences

Work with a partner. Identify what is "bad" about these topic sentences. Are they *questions, announcements* or just *simple facts*? Work together to rewrite these topic sentences.

1. Nine million people live in Tokyo. (Simple fact   )

Tokyo has three places that everyone should see.

2. Today, I will write about my favorite Ghibli movie. (   )

_____

3. What is your favorite season? (   )

_____

4. Do cats dream? (   )

_____

5. This paragraph is about the three most popular sports. (   )

_____

6. People need water to live. (   )

_____

24

THE TOPIC SENTENCE WITH A PREDICTOR

Focus on STRUCTURE Predictors in the Topic Sentence

Topic sentences can also have a **predictor**. Predictors are often included as part of the controlling idea. While controlling ideas limit what you will say about a topic, predictors tell the reader how many major supporting sentences to expect. The highlighted sections below show predictors.

Chocolate is a great dessert because it is sweet, creamy, and nutritious.

Summer is better than winter because of weather, activities, and festivals.

Read the sentences below. Circle the topic and underline the controlling idea. If there is a predictor, draw a square around it. Check your answers with a partner.

1. Teachers can be divided into three types: strict, friendly, and knowledgeable.

2. Paris has some of the best restaurants in the world.

3. It will be a very special day tomorrow.

4. Practice, technique, and playfulness are the three things you need to be good at card tricks.

Note You do not always need to use a predictor, but they can be very helpful to organize your writing.

EXERCISE 3 Build from the Topic Sentence

The topic sentence introduces your topic and what you will write about. In a basic paragraph you should be able to write 2-4 details related to the topic sentence. Using wh-questions can help you think of ideas. Look at the sentence below.

Topic sentence   Orcas eat a variety of other animals.
*(**Which** animals do they eat?)*

Details about the topic   Penguins, seals, other whales

Work with a partner. Look at the topic sentences below and think of 2-4 things you can say about the topic. Did you use a wh-question to help you?

1. Mexico is a great place to travel.
*(**What** great things does Mexico have?)*

   Food, pyramids, beautiful beaches, friendly people

2. College life is much different from life in high school.

(   )

3. The lecture was boring for three reasons.

(   )

4. Music has changed my life in several ways.

(   )

5. There are three tricks to taking great photos.

(   )

THE CONCLUDING SENTENCES

Focus on STRUCTURE Signal, Restate, Summarize, and Leave a Final Message

The concluding sentence(s) are closely related to the topic sentence. It comes at the end of the paragraph and usually does two things. First, it **signals**[1] the end of the paragraph with a signal word or phrase such as *in conclusion* or *in sum*. Second, it **restates**[2] the topic sentence using different words.

Concluding sentences can also **summarize**[3] the major supporting ideas and leave a **final message**[4] for the reader. Look at the example below.

Topic sentence

Taking good photos is not difficult if you follow three easy steps.

Concluding sentence

In conclusion[1], great photos are easy to take[2] if you use good lighting, choose subjects and scenes that you enjoy, and have fun[3]. Enjoy taking great pictures[4]!

When writing concluding sentences (CS), you should use **synonyms** to restate your topic sentence (TS). Synonyms are words and expressions with similar meaning. They give your writing variety and help you avoid repeating words, which can be considered bad style. For example:

TS Travel will **make life more interesting**.
CS In sum, travel **enriches our lives**.

TS There are **three benefits to eating healthy**.
CS Therefore, **eating right can help in three ways**.

EXERCISE 4 · Identify Parts of a Concluding Sentence

Work alone. Which parts of the concluding sentence *signal*, *restate*, *summarize*, and/or *leave a final message*? Then compare your ideas with a partner and discuss what you think the paragraph was about.

1. TS For millions of years, dinosaurs ruled the planet.
   CS In sum, dinosaurs ruled the Earth for a very long time.

2. TS We benefit from hard work in three ways.
   CS All in all, hard work pays off through success, confidence, and perseverance.

3. TS Friends are some of the most important people in our lives.
   CS In conclusion, friends are important because they are fun, supportive, and give you someone to share things with. So, always appreciate your friends.

4. TS There are three winter sports that make winter the most enjoyable time of the year.
   CS Winter sports are a great way to have fun during the cold months.

EXERCISE 5 · Create Concluding Sentences

Work with a partner. Read the topic sentences aloud, then write concluding sentences. Be sure to use synonyms in your concluding sentences. Use the signal words in the box below. Don't forget the comma!

> In conclusion / To sum up / In sum / Therefore

1. The environment can be protected in three easy steps.

   <u>In sum, taking a few steps to save the environment will really help.</u>

2. To learn to play an instrument you must practice, practice, practice.

   _____

3. I think living in the city is better than living in the countryside.

   _____

4. Education should be free to all.

   _____

5. When I was 13 years old, my life changed.

_____

EXERCISE 6 Let's Write

This is a short writing assignment to give you practice with the skills you learned in the first three units.

Write a short paragraph to answer the question below. Use the checklist to help you.

What is the best way to spend summer vacation?

✔ Checklist

- ☐ Each sentence has a subject and a verb.
- ☐ Each sentence can stand alone. It is an independent clause.
- ☐ I capitalized the first letter of each sentence.
- ☐ I capitalized proper names of people, places, and companies.
- ☐ I have punctuation at the end of each sentence.
- ☐ I have both simple sentences and compound sentences.
- ☐ Each compound sentence has a comma and a conjunction.
- ☐ I made compound sentences out of my choppy sentences.
- ☐ I have a clear topic sentence.
- ☐ The topic sentence is a statement, and expresses opinion, intention, or position.
- ☐ There is a predictor in the introduction. _(Optional)_
- ☐ The concluding sentence has a signal and restates my topic sentence.
- ☐ The concluding sentence summarizes the main points and leaves a final message.

✔ Vocabulary Check the words you know, and review the words you do not.

- ☐ Topic sentence
- ☐ Topic
- ☐ Controlling idea
- ☐ Express
  - • Opinion
  - • Intention
  - • Position
- ☐ Concluding sentence (conclusion)
- ☐ Signal
- ☐ Restate
- ☐ Summarize
- ☐ Leave a final message
- ☐ Synonym

BUILDING THE PARAGRAPH

"If you want to change the world, pick up your pen and write."
—Martin Luther

The longest part of any paragraph is the **body**, which is made up of **major** and **minor supporting sentences**. These sentences give all the **details** about the topic and clarify the writer's point of view. The body is also the part of the paragraph that makes a writer's point of view convincing through **explanations**, **examples**, and **anecdotes**.

Topic sentence	This is the topic.
Supporting sentences (Body)	**These are the details.**
Concluding sentence	This was the topic.

THE SUPPORTING SENTENCES

Focus on STRUCTURE Major and Minor Support

The **supporting sentences**, also called the **body**, are the longest part of the paragraph. There are two types of supporting sentences: **major** and **minor**. Major supporting sentences (M) directly support the topic sentence (TS). Minor supporting sentences (m) give support to the major supporting sentences. Look at the example below.

(TS) There are three important steps in taking a great photo.

    (M) First, have good lighting.

        (m) Good lighting is critical for bringing out the details in the photo.

        (m) The lighting should not be too dark or too bright. It should make the subject look clear and focused.

    (M) Second, choose scenes or subjects that interest you.

        (m) When you take photos of things you enjoy, you will stay motivated and use your camera more often.

        (m) For example, maybe you really like to take photos of popular sites, photos of nature, or portraits of people you know. Personally, I like landscapes, but my friend likes to take photos of animals.

Notice that both the major and minor sentences of the body are about the topic of the paragraph.

To write good supporting sentences you need to give details through **explanations**, **examples**, and **anecdotes**.

GIVE EXPLANATIONS

Describe what you mean by asking *wh-questions*. Explanations give **definitions**, **facts**, and other types of **specific information**. Read the example below.

> There are three important steps in taking a great photo.
> → (**What** are the steps?)
> First, have good lighting.
> → (**Why** have good lighting?) → (**What** is "good lighting?")
> Good lighting is critical for bringing out the details in the photo. The lighting should not be too dark or too bright. It should make the subject look clear and focused.

EXERCISE 1 Give Explanations as Supporting Sentences

Work with a partner. Read the sentences and write one wh-question. Then answer the question by writing a supporting sentence. Finally, compare your answer with another pair.

1. One influential writer is Edgar Allan Poe.

*(**Who** is Edgar Allan Poe?)*

　　Edgar Allan Poe was an American writer from the 1800's.

2. Travel is good for us in three ways.

　　(   )

　　_____

3. There are lots of things to do in Tokyo.

　　(   )

　　_____

4. Exercise and a healthy diet are very important.

(   )

_____

5. Writing takes practice.

(   )

_____

GIVE EXAMPLES

Give examples to help the reader **visualize an explanation**. Examples often follow explanations to make them clear and relatable. Examples can be introduced with signals like *for example*, or *for instance*, or with **no signal at all**. Read the example below.

> Second, choose scenes or subjects that interest you. This will help you stay motivated. **For example**, maybe you really like to take photos of **popular sites, photos of nature**, or **portraits of people you know**.

⚠ COMMON ERROR!—Writing examples as fragments

Beginning writers often write examples as fragments. Remember, complete sentences have a subject and a verb. See the examples and corrections below.

✓ Good	✗ Bad
There were many animals. For example, there were cats, dogs, and birds.	There were many animals. For example, cats, dogs, and birds.

EXERCISE 2 Give Examples as Supporting Sentences

Work with a partner. Read the sentences below and write out an example. Be sure you write complete sentences!

1. Different kinds of music affect us differently.

For instance, rock music excites us, but classical is relaxing.
_____

2. There are lots of different hobbies in the world.

_____

3. Sports are very popular all over the world.

_____

4. People do different activities in each of the seasons.

_____

5. We should use good manners when we visit someone's home for the first time.

_____

GIVE ANECDOTES

Give anecdotes to provide a **personal story** or **experience**. Anecdotes are helpful because they connect the writer to the reader in a personal way. Read the example below.

> Second, choose scenes or subjects that interest you. This will help you stay motivated. **Personally, I like landscapes, but my friend likes to take photos of animals**.

EXERCISE 3 Give Anecdotes as Supporting Sentences

Work alone. Read the sentences below. Think of anecdotes and write them down. Then read your answers aloud with a partner.

1. Trying new things helps us grow.

  I went to Canada in high school and learned many new things.

2. Having pets is a big responsibility.

_____

3. Time flies when we are having fun.

_____

33

4. It is important to have goals.

_____

5. A dream job is doing what you love.

_____

STRUCTURE OF A PARAGRAPH

Focus on STRUCTURE The Parts of the Paragraph and What They Do

In review, a **paragraph** is made of three parts: the **topic sentence**, the **supporting sentences**, and the **concluding sentence**.

Remember that the **topic sentence** is the most important sentence in the paragraph. The **supporting sentences** (also called the **body**) give support to your topic sentence. This is the middle section, and it is the longest. The **concluding sentence** (also called the **conclusion**) often restates the topic sentence using **synonyms** to remind the reader of the topic in the paragraph.

EXERCISE 4 Analyze a Model Paragraph

Work alone. Read the paragraph below. Notice how all sentences in the body support the topic sentence. Also, notice how the concluding sentence restates the topic. After reading, work with a partner to answer the questions below.

Topic sentence	A tropical island is the best place to spend summer vacation.
Supporting sentences (Body)	First of all, the white-sand beaches are beautiful. Every day you can sit and watch an amazing sunrise and sunset. Second, you can spend time in the ocean. You can swim with tropical fish, surf, or just play in the waves. Finally, the seafood is super fresh and delicious, and you can eat sushi every day!
Concluding sentence	So, next summer I am going to a tropical island because there is no better place to be.

1. According to the writer, why is a tropical island the best place to spend summer vacation?

2. Can you think of some other reasons?

EXERCISE 5 Read a Model Paragraph

Work with a partner. Take turns reading the model paragraph. Then fill in the outline below.

There are over 4,000 religions worldwide. However, over 50% of people follow one of three popular religions. The first is Christianity. This makes up 31% of the global population. Christians believe that Jesus Christ was the son of God. Islam is the second most popular religion in the world at 24%. Followers are called Muslims. They believe in one God and follow a holy book called the Koran. The third most common religion is called Hinduism. Hinduism is a polytheistic religion. This means they believe in many different gods. Hindus make up over 15% of the world's population. In conclusion, while there are many world religions, a majority of people around the world follow one of these three religions.

Outline

What is the topic?	
What is the controlling idea?	
What is the predictor?	
List supporting details.	
What synonym(s) are used?	

EXERCISE 6 Let's Write

Write a short paragraph to answer the question below. Use the check lists below to help you.

What are the best ways to learn new English vocabulary?

✓ **Checklist**   Unit 4

- ☐ I have a clear topic sentence.
- ☐ The major supporting sentences directly support the topic sentence.
- ☐ The minor supporting sentences give details about major supporting sentences.
- ☐ I have included explanations in my minor supporting sentences.
- ☐ I have included examples in my minor supporting sentences.
- ☐ I have included anecdotes in my minor supporting sentences. *(Optional)*

✓ **Vocabulary**   Check the words you know, and review the words you do not.

- ☐ Body
- ☐ Major supporting sentence
- ☐ Minor supporting sentence
- ☐ Wh-question
- ☐ Explanation
- ☐ Example
- ☐ Anecdote

✓ Checklist   Units 1-3

☐ Each sentence has a subject and a verb.

☐ Each sentence can stand alone. It is an independent clause.

☐ I capitalized the first letter of each sentence.

☐ I capitalized proper names of people, places, and companies.

☐ I have punctuation at the end of each sentence.

☐ I have both simple sentences and compound sentences.

☐ Each compound sentence has a comma and a conjunction.

☐ I made compound sentences out of my choppy sentences.

☐ I have a clear topic sentence.

☐ The topic sentence is a statement, and expresses opinion, intention, or position.

☐ There is a predictor in the introduction. *(Optional)*

☐ The concluding sentence has a signal and restates my topic sentence.

☐ The concluding sentence summarizes the main points and leaves a final message.

EXTRA: ON WRITING

Part 1   APPROACHES TO WRITING

Part 2   FORMATTING YOUR DOCUMENT

How to use this section

Part 1 of this extra unit introduces two common approaches to writing to help you understand the differences between the assignments you will create (**the products**) and the steps you will take to get there (**the process**). You should use Part 1 to develop an understanding that writing is not only about finishing the assignment. While the final assignments are important, you should understand that you are learning to write through a process of writing several **drafts** before handing in your final work.

Part 2 is a guide to **format** your final drafts. It is important that you follow the format correctly so that your writing is easy to read. You should use Part 2 as a reference each time you do an assignment.

Remember, good writing takes time. So, enjoy the process!

Part 1

APPROACHES TO WRITING

"The first draft is just you telling yourself the story." —Terry Pratchett

Writing does not come naturally to most of us. It can be challenging to come up good ideas, find the right vocabulary, and organize our thoughts in an effective way. Moreover, writing assignments, like those found in university classrooms, require us to complete a final written work by a set deadline. As you learn to write better, it is helpful to think about writing in two ways.

 WRITING I

Focus on APPROACH Process versus Product

The product approach to writing focuses on the final work of a writer— the paper you hand in to your teacher to be graded. In this approach, students read **model paragraphs** and try to imitate the organization of those models in a controlled way. This is useful because it helps learners see what their writing should look like when they are finished.

> ✓ Focus on the final paper
> ✓ Focus on model paragraphs
> ✓ Focus on organization
> ✓ Focus on control

The process approach to writing, on the other hand, focuses on the several steps of writing. These steps include planning and **outlining**, writing, **revising, editing**, and **re-writing**. Often, process writing allows students to write and re-write several **drafts**. This approach is helpful because it gives students time to develop the writing and revising skills that will help them be more independent.

> ✓ Focus on the steps of writing
> ✓ Focus on drafts
> ✓ Focus on developing skills
> ✓ Focus on independence

WRITING II

Focus on APPROACH Process and Product

In Units 5-12 of this textbook you will follow both a product and process approach to writing. Each unit presents one or more model paragraphs that you can use to study how a particular type of paragraph can be written. As you begin to write your own drafts, however, you will follow a process approach. That is, you will write, revise, edit and re-write your drafts at least three times before turning in your assignment.

The first draft, which can be either handwritten or typed, should focus on just getting your ideas down on paper. In the first draft, you do not need to worry about grammar and spelling. Just write! After completing the first draft you should take a break. Taking a break is part of the process of writing, and it will help you see your writing with fresh eyes. After returning to your first draft, you will edit and revise based on the lessons from each unit.

The second draft, which will be typed, will be a re-write of your first draft based on edits and revisions you made. You will often share your second draft in class and use class time to ask questions and get feedback from your classmates and teacher. You will also use the lessons in the textbook to further edit and revise for structure, mechanics, and content.

The final draft is your final product that you will turn in to your teacher for grading and feedback. This should be your best work. Final drafts must be typed and correctly formatted.

FORMATTING YOUR DOCUMENT

"Anyone who says that writing is easy isn't doing it right." —Amy Joy

Formatting your document correctly is one of the most important steps in completing assignments. Formatting makes your document easier to read because each section is clear and organized. Below are some general guidelines you should follow when formatting your assignments for Units 5-12.

 FORMATTING

Focus on FORMAT Formatting a Document

In Units 5-12 the final draft of your assignments must be formatted correctly. Study the descriptions and look at the example below.

> [1.]Name
> Class name
> Date
>
> [2.]Title
> [3.]Draft
>
> [4.]Indent the first line using the tab button. [5.]Lines should be double spaced. [6.]The font should be 12pt. [7.]Sentences should be written consecutively and not as a list. [8.]The paragraph should be printed all in black ink. [9.]Print the document on A4 sized paper. [10.]You should use a standard font type such as Times New Roman or Arial.

1. Name, class name and date in upper right-hand corner.

2. Title in the center — 14 to 16-point font.

3. Final draft below title.

4. First line of paragraph indented five spaces.

5. Lines double spaced.

6. Everything in 12-point font except title.

7. Sentences written one after another and not as a list on the page.

8. Black ink only.

9. A4 sized paper only.

10. Standard font type throughout the entire document.

✓ Vocabulary — Check the words you know, and review the words you do not.

☐ The product approach   ☐ Re-writing

☐ The process approach   ☐ First draft

☐ Model paragraph   ☐ Second draft

☐ Outlining   ☐ Final draft

☐ Revising   ☐ Formatting

☐ Editing

PART II

RHETORICAL PATTERNS

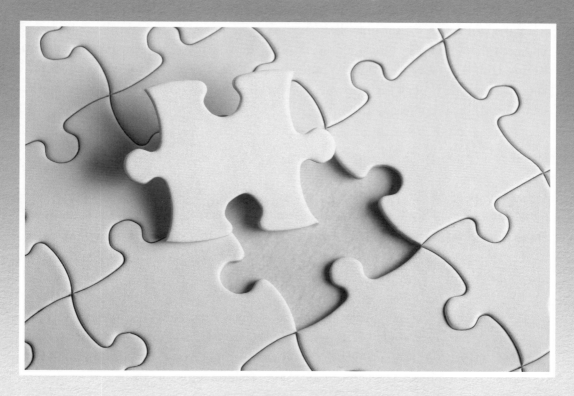

THE PROCESS PARAGRAPH

Unit 5

"Writing is an exploration. You start from nothing." —E.L. Doctorow

1

Now that we have learned about the basic structures of sentences and paragraphs, we can begin writing various types of paragraphs. The first type of paragraph you will write is called a **process paragraph**.

A process paragraph, sometimes called a ***how-to* paragraph**, describes a series of events or actions that one takes to perform a task. A good process paragraph includes predictable steps and details presented in **chronological order** that are easy to follow. When we describe a process, we want to think of the clearest and most logical way to describe each step so that the reader can complete the task successfully.

EXERCISE 1 Read a Model Paragraph

Read the model paragraph. Then work with a partner to answer the questions below.

Picture Perfect

They say, a picture is worth a thousand words. However, taking a great photo is not always easy. There are three important steps in taking a great photo. First, have good lighting. Good lighting is critical for bringing out the details in the photo. The lighting should not be too dark or too bright. It should make the subject look clear and focused. Second, choose scenes or subjects that interest you. When you take photos of things you enjoy, you will stay motivated and use your camera more often. For example, maybe you really like to take photos of popular sites, photos of nature, or portraits of people you know. Personally, I like landscapes, but my friend likes to take photos of animals. Finally, be sure your subject is the focus of your photo. When people look at your photo, your subject should stand out and attract attention. You can do this with lighting, camera angle, and focus. Taking photos is a lot of fun and following these three steps will turn your good photos into great ones.

1. What is the process being described?

2. What is the topic sentence?

3. How many steps are there?

4. What are the steps?

EXERCISE 2 Brainstorm and Discuss

Work with a partner. Make a list of some things you know how to do. Maybe you know how to play a sport or study for exams. Maybe you know how to cook a special dish, make friends, or travel overseas.

- How to play soccer
- How to study for a test
- How to cook omelet rice
- How to make friends
- How to travel overseas
-
-
-
-
-

EXERCISE 3 Describe a Process

Work alone. Choose one of the topics below and write out each step to completing that process. Also, write a topic sentence to introduce your topic. Then work with a partner and read your process aloud.

1. How to get to school

2. How to make a dish

3. How to enjoy summer vacation

4. How to reduce stress

5. How to study for a vocabulary test

OUTLINING MAIN STEPS AND SUPPORTING DETAILS

Focus on ORGANIZATION Creating an Outline

In a process paragraph the topic sentence introduces the process, the major supporting sentences give the **main steps**, and the minor supporting sentences give **supporting details** of each step.

Creating an **outline** will help organize your ideas and make sure you are not missing any main steps in the process. Look at the example of the model paragraph below.

Topic sentence:

There are three important steps in taking a great photo.

Steps	Main Steps	Supporting Details
1	Have good lighting.	Good lighting is critical for bringing out the details in the photo. The lighting should not be…
2	Choose scenes or subjects that interest you.	When you take photos of things you enjoy, you will stay motivated and use your camera more often. For example…
3	Be sure your subject is the focus of your photo.	When people look at your photo, your subject should…

Concluding sentence:

Taking photos is a lot of fun and following these three steps will turn your good photos into great ones.

Notice in the main steps above that there is no **subject** included in the directions. In a process paragraph, each main step begins with an **imperative verb**.

✓ Good	✗ Bad
Have good lighting. **Choose** scenes that interest you.	You have good lighting. You should choose scenes that interest you.

EXERCISE 4 Outline Main Steps and Supporting Details

Work alone. First, fill in the table with the main steps and supporting details for the process you described in Exercise 3. Be sure to use the imperative for the main steps. Include explanations, examples, and anecdotes in the supporting details. Then describe your process to your partner.

Topic sentence:

Steps	Main Steps	Supporting Details
1		
2		
3		

Concluding sentence:

TIME-ORDER WORDS

Focus on COHERENCE Chronological Ordering

Often, process paragraphs include predictable steps in **chronological** order that are easy to follow. Beginning writers often make the error of skipping or not including important steps in the process they are describing.

To describe a process, it is important to use **time-order words** to signal the transition between steps. Time-order words make your writing chronological, meaning that it is arranged according to time.

> **First**, open the package.
> **Second**, remove the contents from the bag.
> **After that**, mix the contents with water, salt, and sugar.
> **Then** heat the mixture in a frying pan.
> **Next**, turn off the heat and let the mixture cool.
> **Finally**, pour the contents into a bowl and enjoy!

Notice that all the time-order words above have a comma except *then*. Also, *finally* is used to signal the last step in the process but is NOT the concluding sentence. You will write your concluding sentence after writing your final step.

You can also use **connectors** like **before** and **after** to link two closely related steps in the process. For example,

> **After** you open the package, remove the contents from the bag.
> Let the mixture cool **before** you pour the contents into a bowl.

Notice that these connectors link two independent clauses. They include a subject and a verb and can stand alone as we learned in Unit 1.

It is perfectly fine to write *first*, *second*, *third*, *fourth*, *finally* for each of the steps in your process. However, the quality and naturalness of your writing will be improved by adding other time-order words, such as *next*, *after that*, *then*, etc. Also, you do not always have to use time-order words for every step. As you write, try different combinations.

⚠ COMMON ERROR!—Skipping steps

Beginning writers often skip steps and assume the reader knows what to do. It is important to include all main steps in the order they occur. Check your partner's instructions in Exercise 3. Were any important steps left out? Could you complete the process?

EXERCISE 5 Identify Steps Using Time-order Words

Work alone. Number the steps below. Then compare your answers with a partner.

Packing for a trip can be easy if you follow these steps.

_____ **a.** Next, collect the items and lay them out so you can see everything clearly.

_____ **b.** You can place your jacket or jumper over the clothes.

_____ **c.** Finally, place your toiletry items toward the top of the bag for easy access.

_____ **d.** After you have what you need, pack the heavy items, like shoes, first.

__1__ **e.** First, make a list of all the things you need to bring on your trip.

_____ **f.** Then pack your clothes on top. Roll or fold your clothes to keep them wrinkle free.

Now, return to Exercise 3, and write in your own time-order words.

EXERCISE 6 Discuss Topics with a Partner

Work with a partner. Discuss topics that interest you. If you cannot think of any topics, you may choose one from the unit. See the list below.

- Describe how to make friends in school.
- Explain how to decorate your room.
- Describe the best way to learn a language.
- Tell how to choose a gift for someone.
- Explain how to get in shape.
- Describe how to have fun with friends without spending any money.

EXERCISE 7 Outline a Process

Work alone. After choosing your topic, write a topic sentence, and begin outlining your main steps and supporting details. (Use the chart below.)

Topic sentence:		
Steps	**Main Steps**	**Supporting Details**
1		
2		
3		
Concluding sentence:		

EXERCISE 8 Let's Write

After you have completed outlining your main steps and supporting details, begin writing your first draft. Remember that this draft does not need to be perfect. Just get your ideas out on paper. You will edit and revise your draft in the next unit.

✓ Vocabulary Check the words you know, and review the words you do not.

☐ Process
☐ How-to paragraph
☐ Chronological order
☐ Main step
☐ Supporting detail

☐ Imperative verb
☐ Time-order word
☐ Connector

THE PROCESS PARAGRAPH

"I could not think without writing." —Jean Piaget

We describe a process using chronological ordering from the first step to the last. Each main step should be followed by supporting details that **highlight** important information. This will make your process easier to understand.

EXERCISE 1 Read a Model Paragraph

Read the model paragraph. Then work with a partner to answer the questions below.

How to Ace the Test

Nobody likes getting a bad grade on a test. To get a good grade, you must study effectively, and there are three steps you need to follow. First, repetition is key. When we learn something new, it is important to have repeated encounters with the new skill or information. This does not mean simply repeating the same thing in the same way. Instead, you should repeat the new information in different ways, for example, by writing it down, reading it out loud, and even teaching someone. Second, don't multitask. Multitasking means doing more than one thing at a time, such as listening to music or using your cellphone while you are trying to study. To study well, you must focus on one thing at a time. Finally, take walks. Taking walks is not only good for your body, but it can also help you learn! Exercise brings more blood flow and oxygen to your brain, which helps improve memory. You must get exercise if you want to improve your learning. So, the next time you are studying for a test, be sure to follow these three easy steps to get your best score ever.

1. What is the process being described?

2. What is the topic sentence?

3. How many steps are there?

4. What are the steps?

Focus on GRAMMAR and MECHANICS Using Modals

In a process paragraph, certain steps will be very important for the reader to be successful. You should **highlight** these steps by using both affirmative and negative modals: **should**, **must**, **should not**, and **must not**.

- **should** for advice
  Subject + **should** + base form of the verb
  First, open the package. **You should open** it slowly, so you do not make a mess.

- **must** for necessity
  Subject + **must** + base form of the verb
  First, check the power source. **You must check** that it has batteries.

- **should not** for warning
  Subject + **should not** + base form of the verb
  First, open the package. **You should not open** the package too quickly.

- **must not** for prohibition
  Subject + **must not** + base form of the verb
  Next, pour the contents into a bowl. **You must not use** a plate.

Notice how each of the main steps above is a complete sentence in the imperative with no subject and does not use a modal verb. Do not use modals in the main step.

⚠ COMMON ERROR!——Using modals with incorrect verb forms

Beginning writers often use modals with incorrect verb forms. When writing your process paragraph, **only use modals with the base form of the verb**.

EXERCISE 2 Find and Fix Modal Errors in a Paragraph

Work alone. Read the excerpt below. Underline each modal error, then rewrite the sentence correctly. The first error has been underlined and re-written. There are five errors remaining. Finally, compare your answers with a partner.

Everyone wants to get better at something, but what is the most effective way to improve? To get better at just about anything, follow these three steps. First, <u>you should write out your goal</u>. Writing the goal helps you identify what you want to achieve. You should writing your goal in a notebook or journal so you can reviewing it later. Second, you should make a five-step plan for achieving this goal. You must being realistic and thinking about what you need to get started. Next,...

1. First, write out your goal.

2. _____

3. _____

4. _____

5. _____

6. _____

EXERCISE 3 Highlight Important Steps

Work with a partner. Read the topic and include an important step using a modal verb. Try to write both *affirmative* and *negative* sentences.

1. Taking a test

   You should answer the easy questions first.

   You must not cheat!

2. Driving

   _____

   _____

3. Watching a movie at the cinema

   _____

   _____

4. Visiting someone's house for the first time

_____

_____

5. Using your cellphone

_____

_____

EXERCISE 4 Edit Your Process Paragraph

Work alone. Look at the process paragraph you wrote for Unit 5. Highlight important supporting details by using modals. Then exchange papers with a partner and help each other edit.

GETTING THE READER'S ATTENTION

Focus on MECHANICS Adding a Hook

Sometimes process paragraphs can sound very mechanical, like simply reading a set of instructions. However, there are two ways to make the writing more interesting and meaningful. The first is to add a **hook** at the beginning of the paragraph to draw the attention of the reader to your topic.

Look at the excerpt below from the model paragraph in Unit 5, page 46. Notice that the first two sentences are _not_ the topic sentence.

> They say, a picture is worth a thousand words. However, taking a great photo is not always easy. There are three important steps in taking a great photo.

In the first two sentences, the writer introduced the topic to the readers in an interesting way before writing the topic sentence. These sentences are called a hook. A hook is a general sentence or two _about_ the topic but is not the topic sentence itself. Read the examples below.

1. Hook Have you ever seen a ghost?
Topic sentence Last year I had a very scary experience.

2. Hook Everyone loves movies. Each movie genre can take us to a new world.
Topic sentence The three best movie genres are action, horror, and suspense.

As you begin to write your process paragraph, include a hook. It will improve the quality of your writing, make it smooth and natural, and motivate the reader to continue reading your paragraph. The examples below are all paragraphs about 'dreams' introduced to the reader using different hooks.

- A hook can be a **famous quote:**

   Martin Luther King Jr. said, "I have a dream."

- A **question:**

   Do cats dream?

- A **general statement** about the topic introducing it in an interesting way:

   We can learn a lot from our dreams.

EXERCISE 5 Work with Hooks

Work with a partner. Read the example topic sentences below. Try to think of an interesting hook by writing either a *famous quote*, a *question*, or a *general statement about the topic*.

1. Anyone can improve their English writing by following these steps.

   Do you want to improve your English writing?

2. Cleaning your room is very easy if you follow these three easy steps.

_____

3. There are five steps to having a great party.

_____

4. We can all help protect the environment if we do these four things.

_____

5. We can all make new friends if we follow these simple steps.

_____

EXERCISE 6 Edit Your Draft

Work alone. Look at your process paragraph, and add a hook before the topic sentence. Then share your paragraph with a partner by reading it aloud.

EXERCISE 7 Let's Write

Write the final draft of a process paragraph. Include all that you have learned in Units 5 and 6. Use the checklist below for help.

✔ Checklist

- ☐ I included all main steps.
- ☐ I included supporting details.
- ☐ I included a hook.
- ☐ I included time-order words.
- ☐ I used the imperative for the main steps.
- ☐ I did not use a subject for my main steps.
- ☐ I did not use a modal in the main steps.
- ☐ I used a subject with each modal.
- ☐ I used the base form of the verb with modals.

✔ Formatting

- ☐ I properly formatted my paragraph.
  - ☐ Name, class, date
  - ☐ Title and draft
  - ☐ Indented first line
  - ☐ Double spaced
  - ☐ 12-point font except title

Unit 7

THE DESCRIPTIVE PARAGRAPH

"Don't tell me the moon is shining, show me the glint of light on broken glass." —Bernard Cornwell

Descriptive paragraphs describe someone or something by using **sensory details** to help the reader *see, smell, hear, taste,* and *touch* what the writer is describing. The purpose of description is not simply to give a definition of an object but to create an image in the reader's mind by using **adjectives** to paint an accurate picture.

EXERCISE 1 Describe the Pictures

Look at the pictures. Work with a partner to describe what you see. Then answer the questions below.

A.

B.

C.

- What can you hear in each picture?
- What can you smell in each picture?
- What can you taste in each picture?
- What can you feel/touch in each picture?

Read the model paragraph. Then work with a partner and answer the questions below.

A Picture of Happiness

One of my most precious possessions is a childhood photograph of my friends and me. The picture was taken when I was 13 years old. We went camping that summer, and we had so much fun. In the photo, I am standing with my two best friends in front of Lake Yamanaka. On my right is my friend Yuta. He is the tallest. He has a big smile on his face, and he is holding a trout that he caught from the lake. On my left is Kazuto. He is the shortest of us all. He is making a funny face and looking at Yuta. I am standing in the middle laughing. In the photo we are all wearing colorful swim shorts and our skin is dark brown from the sun. Our hair is wet because we were swimming all day in the cold blue water. We are all barefoot in the photo, and I remember the small, black stones were painful on our feet, but we still ran and played all day without shoes. That night we had a barbeque. The smell of woodsmoke and grilled fish filled the air. We ate by the fire, and it was delicious. Every time I look at that photograph, I remember the good times we had on that camping trip. That is why the photograph is so special to me.

1. What is the possession?

2. How does the writer feel about the possession?

3. Where and when did the writer get the possession?

4. Why is the possession important to the writer?

ADJECTIVE TYPES

Focus on GRAMMAR Adjectives of Quantity and Quality

Description relies heavily on the use of adjectives. There are two types of adjectives that are particularly important when learning to write descriptive paragraphs.

Adjectives give us information about nouns. First, they tell us about the **quantities** of nouns (how much or how many). Adjectives that describe quantities always come before the noun they are describing.

> a **million** dollars
> **many** people
> Snow White and the **Seven** Dwarfs.

Adjectives also describe the **qualities** and **states** of nouns. These **descriptive adjectives** often go directly before the noun they are describing.

> the **fast** runner
> an **amazing** sunset
> **kind** words

EXERCISE 3 Use Adjectives for Quantities and Qualities

Work alone. Choose the best adjective from the box below to complete the sentence. More than one answer may be possible. Then compare your answers with a partner.

~~hardworking~~	interesting	a lot of	serious
seven thousand	funny	gold	many

1. She is a hardworking person.

2. I don't have _____ time to talk right now.

3. This is a _____ problem.

4. There were _____ people at the concert.

5. He wore a fancy _____ watch.

6. Everyone laughed when he told the_____ story.

7. We watched a very _____ movie in class the other day.

MORE DESCRIPTIVE ADJECTIVES

Focus on GRAMMAR Using Linking Verbs

Adjectives do not always go directly before the nouns they modify. Sometimes adjectives come after the noun. For these types of descriptions, we need to use linking verbs.

Descriptive adjectives can also come directly after a **linking verb**, which sits between a noun and an adjective.

> The water **is** warm.
> The food **tastes** sweet.
> His shirt **looks** good.

There are several common linking verbs. The most common is the **be verb**. It describes the state of something directly. Other linking verbs, such as **sense verbs**, describe how something **looks**, **sounds**, **tastes**, **smells**, **feels**, or **seems** to someone.

Compare:

> The curry **is** hot.   → The curry **looks** hot.
> She **is** friendly.   → She **seems** friendly.
> That **is** French.   → That **sounds** French.

Each of the first sentences expresses greater certainty. The second sentences describe sensory details with lesser certainty.

EXERCISE 4 Use Adjectives with Linking Verbs

Work alone. Use the linking verbs and the adjectives in the boxes below to make sentences. Be sure to change the form of the verb if necessary. More than one answer may be possible. Then compare your answers with a partner.

Linking Verbs	be	taste	look	smell	seem	sound	feel
Adjectives	delicious	angry	new	soft	friendly	beautiful	sweet

1. The food <u>smells delicious</u> .
2. The dog _____ .
3. Our new neighbor _____ .
4. Her singing _____ .
5. The water _____ .
6. The grass _____ .
7. His car _____ .

EXERCISE 5 Brainstorm and Discuss

Work with a partner. Think of some possessions that are important to you and make a list. Then share your ideas with the class.

EXERCISE 6 Let's Write

Begin writing the first draft of a descriptive paragraph. Use the model paragraph in this unit as an example. Write as much as you can about your item. Be sure to answer these four questions.

1. What is the possession?
2. How do you feel about the possession?
3. Where and when did you get the possession?
4. Why is the possession important to you?

Vocabulary Check the words you know, and review the words you do not.

- [ ] Description
- [ ] Sensory detail
- [ ] Adjective
- [ ] Quantity
- [ ] Quality
- [ ] Linking verb

THE DESCRIPTIVE PARAGRAPH

"You can't edit a blank page." —Nora Roberts

To write an effective descriptive paragraph, **adjective order** and the use of **specific language** are critical for creating an accurate image in the reader's mind. Additionally, when describing an object, we often do so in a way that is easy to follow, such as from left to right, top to bottom, and so on. This systematic approach is called **spatial ordering** because it describes how something looks in space.

 **EXERCISE 1 Read a Model Paragraph**

Read the model paragraph. Then work with a partner to answer the questions below.

The Treasure of Time

I have a watch that is very special to me. I received it from my grandfather when I graduated high school. That day, he came to me, said congratulations, and handed me a small black box. He said, "Time is a precious thing. Use it wisely." I opened the box, and inside was an antique gold watch that my grandfather had worn when he was a young man. I love this watch because of the details in it. The clear glass face lets me see the gears and cogs spinning inside. The hour and minute hands of the watch are black. They are made of thin, delicate metal. The red second hand moves efficiently past the Roman numerals on the dial. The watch is attached to a dark leather strap, which my grandfather chose for me. The watch is Swiss-made, and it is heavy on my wrist. I like the feeling of the weight. To keep time, I must spin the crown to wind up the gears each morning. Once the gears are wound up, there is a beautiful soft tick, and it keeps perfect time. Even though I like the way this old watch looks, I love it because it was given to me by my grandfather and reminds me every day of his important words.

1. How does the writer feel about the watch?

2. Where/when did the writer get the watch?

3. Can you describe the watch to your partner?

4. Why is the watch important to the writer?

USING ADJECTIVES EFFECTIVELY

Focus on STRUCTURE Adjective Order

English has an appropriate adjective order that is important to follow when describing nouns. While changing the order is not grammatically incorrect, it just sounds "wrong" to native English users and makes reading more difficult.

Study the chart below and notice the way the adjectives are ordered before the noun. The best way to get used to adjective order in English is to read a lot and write a lot. For now, you can use the chart to help you write your descriptions. Take turns reading the clauses out loud with a partner.

Number	Opinion	Age	Color	Origin	Material	Purpose	Noun
	beautiful		green				gem
three		old			cotton		T-shirts
		new		Italian		sports	car
five	amazing		black	French	wooden		boxes
	comfortable		purple			sleeping	bag

*See Appendix for full adjective order. ❨ ➡ Page 102 ❩

EXERCISE 2 Correct Adjective Order

Work alone. Read the sentences below. Rewrite the sentences with correct adjective order. Then compare your answers with a partner.

1. He bought yellow new shoes.

   He bought new yellow shoes.

2. She had a heart-shaped beautiful gold Egyptian locket.

_____

3. The rusty little old rowboat.

_____

4. She has brown wavy long hair.

_____

5. The house old wooden dark was scary at night.

_____

EXERCISE 3 Make Notes on Your Special Possession

Work alone. Make notes on your special possession. Try to include as much detail as you can. Then share your notes with your partner.

What is the item?	
How do you feel about the item?	
When did you get the item?	
Where did you get the item?	
What is the… • Size • Shape • Age • Color • Origin • Material • Purpose	
How and why is it important?	

CREATING A DETAILED IMAGE

Focus on LANGUAGE Specific Language and Sensory Details

When describing something, be as specific as possible. This means using concrete nouns as well as adjectives to create a detailed image. To do this, you may need to do a little research to find the correct vocabulary.

Look at the details in the sentences taken from the model paragraph.

> **The red second hand** moves efficiently past **the Roman numerals** on **the dial**. The watch is **Swiss-made**, and it is **heavy on my wrist**.

The writer describes the watch using color, weight, parts of the watch, and even where the watch was made. The writer is very specific about the description so that the reader can see the watch clearly in their mind. Look at the example sentences below. See how they have been edited to include more specific detail.

The room was crowded.
→ The room was full of people, and it was hard to move.

It was big.
→ It was the size of a small car.

⚠ COMMON ERROR!——Not being specific enough

Beginning writers often fail to be detailed enough about what they are describing. It is important to be as accurate as possible and include as much specific language as you can so that the reader can see what you are describing. As you help your partner edit his/her draft, be sure you ask questions about the item he/she is describing. Can you see its size, shape, color, material, and so on? If not, encourage them to add more specific language.

EXERCISE 4 Add Sensory Details

Work with a partner. Rewrite the sentences using specific language for sensory details. Be creative. Remember to follow correct adjective order.

1. I watched the sunset.

   I watched the fiery golden-red sunset over high mountain peaks.

2. The ice cream was delicious.

   _____

3. She listened to music.

   _____

4. We smelled food.

   _____

5. The sofa was soft.

   _____

6. The house was dark.

   _____

ORGANIZING THE DESCRIPTION

Focus on COHERENCE Spatial Ordering

Another important aspect of description is doing it in a way that helps the reader "see" it. Depending on the object, it is best to start at a single point on the object and describe it as it is seen in space, such as from top to bottom, left to right, or from front to back.

EXERCISE **5** Recognize Spatial Ordering

Read the short description. Then answer the questions below.

My Precious Friend

My stuffed rabbit, Jana, is so important to me because I have had her since I was a baby. Her soft floppy ears are long. The insides are white, while the outsides are a light brown. They hang down on the sides of her face. She has two shiny black eyes and a small black nose. Her arms reach out to the sides revealing two soft white paws. Her feet are white and round, and she has a big furry belly.

A.

B.

C.

1. Which picture is the writer describing?

2. How does the writer order the description? From left to right? Top to bottom?

3. Which words helped you know which picture was being described?

EXERCISE 6 — Let's write

Write the final draft of your descriptive paragraph. Include all that you have learned in Units 7 and 8. Use the checklist below for help.

✓ Checklist

- ☐ My topic sentence introduced an important item.
- ☐ I expressed how I feel about the item.
- ☐ I used a variety of adjectives in my descriptions.
- ☐ I used linking verbs correctly.
- ☐ I used sense verbs.
- ☐ I followed the correct adjective order in my descriptions.
- ☐ I used specific language for sensory details in my descriptions.
- ☐ I used spatial ordering to organize my descriptions.
- ☐ My paragraph is formatted correctly.

THE NARRATIVE PARAGRAPH

"You are what you write." —Helvy Tiana Rosa

A **narrative paragraph** describes an **experience** that happened in the past. Narratives are like stories and usually center around a single, main event. Just like other types of paragraphs, narratives have a topic sentence, a body, and a concluding sentence. In a narrative paragraph, the topic sentence gives **background information** and introduces the topic. The body includes the main details of the story and has a **beginning, middle** and **end**. The concluding sentence often restates the topic sentence or tells the reader what the writer learned from the experience.

EXERCISE 1 Read a Model Paragraph

Read the model paragraph. Then work with a partner to answer the questions below.

An Embarrassing Day at School

Something embarrassing happened to me when I was a junior high school student. It was the first day of school, and I didn't know the campus very well. I was walking to the cafeteria for lunch when I needed to use the restroom. I saw one up ahead and walked in without looking at the sign. After walking in, I realized I had made a big mistake. I was in the wrong restroom! I looked up and saw a group of older girls there. They were laughing and pointing at me. They told me that the boy's room was on the other side of the hall! I couldn't speak. My face turned bright red, and my mouth was hanging wide open as I turned around and walked out. As I walked into the boy's restroom across the hall, I could still hear the girls laughing at me. This was one of the most embarrassing days of my life, but I learned to always check the sign before walking into a restroom.

1. What is the topic sentence?

2. What is the main event that happened?

3. What happened before the event?

4. What is the concluding sentence?

5. What did the writer learn?

TALKING ABOUT PAST EXPERIENCES AND EVENTS

Focus on GRAMMAR The Simple Past and Past Progressive (was/were + -ing)

When we talk about the past, we often do so by describing both single points in time and actions that were happening at those times. This kind of description creates a vivid picture for our reader.

In narrative paragraphs, we tell a story about events that happened in the past. To do this, we use the **simple past** and **past progressive**. These tenses are used in relation to how they communicate the way events and actions happened in time.

- The simple past describes **specific events** as **single, short points in time**.

    The door **opened**. (The door opened once, at a single point in time.)

- The past progressive *(was/were + -ing)* gives '**background**' information **over longer periods of time**.

    She **was thinking** about her friend. (Thinking happens over time.)

- The past progressive is often used together with the simple past to give background information to specific events.

    She **was thinking** about her friend when the door **opened**.

• The simple past interrupts or happens during the past progressive.

She **was thinking** about her friend when the door **opened**.

	x

past   ← event over time →   single point   *now*

EXERCISE 2 Identify the Simple Past and Past Progressive ◉

Work alone. Return to the model paragraph on page 71 and underline the past progressive. Then circle the simple past tense verb. Finally, compare your answers with a partner.

CONNECTING EVENTS AND FOCUSING THE READER

Focus on GRAMMAR Complex Sentences and Subordinating Conjunctions

Another important feature of narrative paragraphs is writing **complex sentences**. A complex sentence connects an independent and dependent clause with a **subordinating conjunction**. While there are many subordinating conjunctions, the ones listed below are the most common in a narrative paragraph.

Subordinating Conjunctions

when	before	after	until	while

We often use subordinating conjunctions together with the simple past and past progressive to show how two events are connected in *time*.

When the phone rang, I was sitting on my bed.

The clause with the subordinating conjunction can go either first or last in the sentence. When the dependent clause is first, a comma separates the two clauses.

When the phone rang, I was sitting on my bed.

When the dependent clause is second, there is no comma.

I was sitting on my bed **when** the phone rang.

73

Complex sentences using subordinating conjunctions also tell the reader where to **focus**. The focus of your narrative, and what the reader **expects**, are created in the second part of the sentence. Therefore, in the sentence,

> When the phone rang, **I was sitting on my bed**.

the reader is focused on you sitting on the bed. Whereas in the sentence,

> I was sitting my bed **when the phone rang**.

the reader is focused on the phone call.

EXERCISE 3 Find Subordinating Conjunctions

Work alone. Read the model paragraph. Underline the past progressive, draw a square around subordinating conjunctions, and circle the simple past tense verb. Then compare your answers with a partner. Discuss how the subordinating conjunctions connect the past progressive and simple past. Notice what information the writer is focusing on as the most important information.

An Amazing Experience

Last year I had an amazing experience. I was sitting in my room when my mother called me into the kitchen. She told me we were going to Hawaii! I was very excited because I had always wanted to go. We flew to Hawaii the next week. While we were there, we swam in the ocean a lot. On the third day, my father said we were going snorkeling with whale sharks! We took a boat out to sea, put on our snorkels, and jumped in the water. The deep blue ocean looked bottomless, and the water felt cool on my skin. We were swimming around when suddenly we saw a giant whale shark coming up from below. At first, I was scared because it was so big and powerful. It was the size of a city bus, but it moved very slowly. My mother was diving down and taking pictures while I swam on the surface. The whale shark was eating krill, and it opened its huge mouth, which looked like a tunnel. Soon the whale shark swam away. We watched it swim slowly away until it disappeared into the deep blue ocean. After returning home, I told my friends about my amazing experience. I hope that one day I can do it again.

⚠ COMMON ERROR!—Using verb tense inconsistently

When writing a narrative paragraph, you must have a consistent tense. Since narratives are written in the simple past and past progressive, you must be sure that each sentence is written this way. If not, the grammar and writing will be confusing and difficult to follow. Return to model paragraph in this unit. Notice how each of the verbs are in the past tense.

EXERCISE 4 Write Complex Sentences

Work alone. Connect the two independent clauses with a subordinating conjunction. Be sure to use a comma when needed.

1. She was cooking dinner. They arrived. (When)

She was cooking dinner when they arrived.

When they arrived, she was cooking dinner.

2. We sat and talked. The children played. (While)

_____

_____

3. They got home. The package arrived. (Before)

_____

_____

4. I checked my email. I came home. (After)

_____

_____

5. We are not allowed to leave. We hear the bell. (Until)

_____

_____

EXERCISE 5 Find Inconsistent Verb Tense

Work alone. Read the model paragraph. Underline each verb. Then correct the verb tense if there is an error.

My First Bike

On my 15th birthday, I ~~receive~~ the best gift ever. I wake up that morning
received
and I am very excited. My father says he has a big surprise for me after lunch.

Then he leaves the house. I cannot wait. My mother makes lunch, and we sit

down to eat. My father is still not home. After lunch, my father comes into the

kitchen and asks if I am ready for the surprise. I jump up and tell him I am

ready. He takes me outside and sitting in front of the house is my new bike. It

was red and white and had many gears. I am so excited. I get on my new bike,

and I ride all day. I feel so free riding fast with the wind blowing in my hair.

I ride on the street and in the dirt and everywhere in my neighborhood. I love

that bike and ride it almost every day. My 15th birthday is a really great day.

EXERCISE 6 **Brainstorm and Discuss**

Work with a partner. Think of some memorable experiences in your lives and add to the list below. Then share your ideas with the class.

- A person that inspired you
- The best/worst trip ever
- The first day of school

EXERCISE 7 **Let's Write**

Choose one of the topics above and begin writing your first draft about a memorable experience. Use the model paragraphs and the lessons in this unit to help you.

✓ Vocabulary — Check the words you know, and review the words you do not.

- ☐ Narrative
- ☐ Experience
- ☐ Background information
- ☐ Simple past
- ☐ Past progressive

- ☐ Complex sentence
- ☐ Subordinating conjunction
- ☐ Inconsistent verb tense

THE NARRATIVE PARAGRAPH

"Write what you know." —Mark Twain

2

A common feature of narrative paragraphs is the type of details used to describe an experience. In Units 7 and 8 we used description to give details about a special possession. In a narrative paragraph, we use description to help the reader feel and sense the events that happened in the story we are telling. In order to do this, we must use both **sensory** and **emotional details** to bring the experience to life.

EXERCISE 1 Read a Model Paragraph

Read the model paragraph. Then work with a partner to answer the questions below.

My Happy Place

When I was a kid, my favorite place was the park near my house. Every day after school my friends and I would go to the park and play. We would run and laugh under the hot sun. We would climb the tall green trees that stretched high into the sky and listen while the wind blew the leaves on the branches. When we played hide-and-go-seek, my favorite place to hide was behind the bushes with the beautiful pink and purple flowers. They smelled sweet, and sometimes I would stay there even after the game was finished. In the summer, there were many kids playing in that park. We could hear laughing and screaming all day as kids played different games. Sometimes my family had picnics and barbecues there. We ate delicious chicken and juicy watermelon and drank cold drinks while we sat on the cool grass. Everyone was smiling and peaceful. My mother said these are some of her best memories. The park near my house is a really great place. I will never forget the wonderful times I had there.

1. What is the topic sentence?

2. What did the writer do with friends in the park?

3. How does the writer describe the trees?

4. What does the writer hear in the park in the summertime?

5. What did the writer do at the picnics and barbecues?

6. How did people feel when they were in the park?

DESCRIPTIONS IN THE NARRATIVE PARAGRAPH

Focus on STRUCTURE Describing Sensory and Emotional Experience

Just like in descriptive paragraphs from Units 7 and 8, we should include **sensory details** in narratives to help the reader *see, smell, hear, taste,* and *touch* the details in the story.

> I saw a big, wet, fluffy black dog.
> The kitchen smelled like cinnamon, hot apple pie, and vanilla ice cream.
> It was raining, and the wind blew very cold.

However, narrative paragraphs also include details about how the writer felt about certain situations. These descriptions help the reader understand the emotional experience of the writer and make the narrative more interesting. These are called **emotional details**.

> I felt excited to get to work.
> In the dark room I felt lonely and afraid.
> The interview started, and my hands were shaking.

These sentences help the reader feel the emotions of the writer. One feels hopeful, one feels scared and one feels nervous.

EXERCISE 2 Add Emotional Detail

Work with a partner. Read each sentence. Then write a sentence with emotional details.

1. I waited for the interview.

   I felt nervous, and my legs were shaking.

2. I got the job!

3. I took a big bite of my sandwich before I noticed it was moldy and rotten.

4. It rained every day for a month.

5. I stood at the door of the airplane with my parachute on, ready to jump out.

QUOTING DIALOGUE WITH DIRECT AND INDIRECT QUOTES

Focus on MECHANICS Speech in Narratives

Another way to give details in a narrative paragraph is to **quote dialogue** with **direct** and **indirect quotes**.

We use **direct quotes** when we are writing exactly what someone said.

> I asked, "Do you like music?"
> She said, "I love music!"

Notice that the punctuation is always inside the quotation mark.

We use **indirect quotes** when we cannot remember the exact words a person used.

> Original quote "I walk my dog every morning."
> Indirect quote He said he walks his dog in the morning.

Notice that the pronouns have changed from the direct to the indirect quote.

I walk **my** dog every morning. → **He** walks **his** dog in the morning.

⚠ COMMON ERROR!——Mixing direct and indirect quotes

When quoting dialogue, you must pay attention to the use of personal pronouns (I, you, he, she, etc.) and possessive pronouns (my, your, his, her, etc.) These pronouns will affect the meaning of the quote and of the whole sentence. Read this common error.

Original quote "My favorite place is my room."
Indirect quote Yuta said his favorite place was **my** room. (incorrect)

Is Yuta's favorite place the writer's room? No, the writer made a mistake by mixing a direct quote and an indirect quote and did not change the pronoun.

Indirect quote Yuta said his favorite place was **his** room. (correct)

EXERCISE 3 Write Direct and Indirect Quotes

Interview a partner. Ask the questions below and listen to their exact quotes. First, write direct quotes. Then write them as indirect quotes.

1. Where was your favorite place when you were a child?
Ex. Yuta said, "My room." → Yuta said it was his room.

2. What was your favorite animal?

3. What games did you like in elementary school?

4. What was your favorite day of the week? Why?

PRONOUN-ANTECEDENT AGREEMENT

Focus on GRAMMAR Tracking Pronoun-antecedent Relationships

An **antecedent** is the noun (or pronoun) to which another **pronoun** refers. For example, in the sentence:

> **Miyuki** thinks **she** will be late for class.
>
> (*Miyuki* is the antecedent and *she* is the pronoun that refers to Miyuki.)

Pronoun-antecedent agreement is critical for producing quality writing. Beginning writers often make mistakes with pronoun-antecedent agreement both within sentences:

> While studying, **you** sit down for a long time, and **my** blood flow gets worse.

And between them:

> Even if **we** have a big test the next day, **you** must take a break and get light exercise. This will help **my** learning and **I** will do better on the test.

Can you find the errors above?

As you develop your writing skills, it is important to keep track of pronoun-antecedent relationships to make sure that they are consistent both within and between sentences.

EXERCISE 4 Find and Correct Pronoun-antecedent Errors

Work alone. Read the sentences and circle the pronoun-antecedent errors. Then re-write the sentence. Finally, compare your answers with a partner.

1. (Writers) should always pay attention to (your) use of pronouns in sentences.

Writers should always pay attention to their use of pronouns in sentences.

2. My mother said these are some of my best memories.

_____

3. Mr. Fukushima wants me to turn his final draft in by tomorrow afternoon.

_____

4. You and I must study harder before my exams next week.

_____

5. Some of the cars had its windows down in the rain last night.

_____

EXERCISE 5 Let's Write

Write the final draft of a narrative paragraph. Include all that you have learned in Units 9 and 10. Use the checklist below for help.

✓ Checklist

- ☐ My topic sentence gave background information.
- ☐ My topic sentence introduced the topic.
- ☐ I used the simple past tense.
- ☐ I used the past progressive tense.
- ☐ I used subordinating conjunctions.
- ☐ I wrote complex sentences.
- ☐ The past tense is consistent.
- ☐ I wrote sensory details.
- ☐ I wrote emotional details.
- ☐ I wrote direct and indirect quotes correctly.
- ☐ I have pronoun-antecedent agreement.
- ☐ My paragraph is formatted correctly.

THE OPINION PARAGRAPH

"A word after a word after a word is power." —Margaret Atwood

In an opinion paragraph, the writer expresses an **opinion** about a topic and then supports that opinion with **facts**, **explanations**, **examples**, and **anecdotes**. The writer also considers the **counter-argument**. The purpose of an opinion paragraph is to get the reader to agree with the writer's view. Therefore, the writer must present **reasons** in a way that seems logical and well supported. Being able to express and support opinions well is at the core of strong academic writing.

EXERCISE 1 Read a Model Paragraph

Read the model paragraph. Then work with a partner to answer the questions below.

Anti-social Media

Nowadays, everyone is on social media. But is it really good for us? In my opinion, social media is harmful to society. To begin with, it is a waste of time. On average, people spend over two hours per day on social media. That time could be spent pursuing goals and dreams, spending time with friends and family, or actually doing the things people are watching on social media! Second, social media is hurting our bodies. People who use their smartphones too much get bad eyes and often have neck and shoulder pain. This is because they are staring at a screen for hours with their necks hunched forward. This damage to the body is not worth it. Finally, social media makes people feel lonely. While some may think they are connecting more with their friends on social media, they most likely communicate less face-to-face because they communicate with text messages, comments, and likes instead. They also spend time comparing their lives to the lives of other people, which can make them feel isolated. When I see people posting on social media, they always look like they have amazing lives. It makes me feel like my life is boring, and I start to feel bad. All in all, for the reasons stated above, social media is bad for society.

1. What is the topic sentence?

2. What is the writer's opinion?

3. How many reasons does the writer give to support his/her opinion?

4. What are the reasons?

5. What is the concluding sentence?

6. What does the title mean?

7. Do you think social media is good or bad for society? Why?

INTRODUCING AN OPINION

Focus on STRUCTURE Clarity and Singularity

An opinion paragraph, like all other paragraphs, begins with the **topic sentence**. The topic sentence should express a single opinion on **a single topic**. A writer may also choose to include a predictor.

Topic sentence
In my opinion, **social media** is harmful to society (for three reasons).
Single topic   **social media**
Single Opinion   is harmful to society
Predictor   (for three reasons)

There are **three common problems** when writing the topic sentence for opinion paragraphs.

· It is **an announcement**.

    Today, I will write about social media.

- It is **too general**.

  Social media is bad.

- It is **too specific**.

  Social media is a kind of social networking site on the internet.

Remember a **"good" topic sentence should express an opinion, intention, statement, or position** on a single topic. (See Unit 3, page 23)

In an opinion paragraph, **a hook** is often used before the topic sentence to introduce the topic and get the reader's attention. (See Unit 6, page 56)

  Nowadays, everyone is on social media. But is it really good for us?

EXERCISE 2 Correct Topic Sentence Problems

Work with a partner. Read the topic sentences below. Discuss whether you think they are *announcements, too general, too specific,* or *good topic sentences*. Revise the sentences that have problems.

1. Shopping is fun. (Too general   )

   Shopping is a great way to spend the day.

2. I will write my opinion of soccer in the following paragraph. (   )

_____

3. Chocolate is made from cacao. (   )

_____

4. There are three ways healthy eating will improve your life. (   )

_____

5. Music is good. (   )

_____

86

CONVINCING YOUR READER

Focus on STRUCTURE Types of Supporting Details

The most important part of an opinion paragraph is the supporting detail found in the major and minor supporting sentences. This is where you try to convince your reader to agree with your point of view by using a combination of **explanations**, **examples**, and **anecdotes**. (See Unit 4, page 31)

Additionally, it is a good idea to provide **facts** to support your opinion. Facts will give your opinion the strongest support because they are true for everyone. To help you generate ideas for facts and explanations, you can ask yourself: *How do I know?*

- **Facts** — knowledge and information that are generally true for everyone

  People waste time on social media. → *(How do I know?)*
  → On average, people spend over two hours per day on social media. That equals one month on social media per year!

- **Explanations** — details and descriptions that help make a statement clear

  Social media is hurting our bodies. → *(How do I know?)*
  → People who use their smartphones too much get bad eyes and often have neck and shoulder pain. This is because they are staring at a screen for hours with their necks hunched forward.

To support your opinion with examples and anecdotes you can ask yourself: *How can I show this?*

- **Examples** — a sample that shows what the writer means

  Social media platforms → *(How can I show this?)*
  → , for example, when people read postings on Facebook and TikTok, they often end up comparing their lives to those of other people.

The above example shows the reader what the writer means by social media. The writer could have chosen any social media platforms but limited the example to Facebook and TikTok.

- **Anecdotes** — a personal example or story about you or someone you know

> People waste time on social media. → *(How can I show this?)*
> → I spend hours watching YouTube videos every day.

The above anecdote is a personal story used to connect to the reader because many people spend a great deal of time on YouTube and other social media platforms.

While it is not necessary to include all types of support, it is a good idea to use a combination of these different types. A common problem is giving examples too soon. Generally, it is better to give facts and explanations before giving examples.

EXERCISE 3 Identify Types of Supporting Details

Work with a partner. Read the supporting sentences below. Decide if it is a *fact*, *explanation*, *example*, or *anecdote*.

1. In London it rains nearly 100 days a year. (Fact)

2. K2 in Pakistan is the second highest mountain in the world. ( )

3. In Kyoto there are lots of great places to visit, such as temples, shrines and restaurants. ( )

4. My best friend used to live in New York. ( )

5. If we learn another language, we will be able to communicate with people from other parts of the world. This can broaden our lives and experiences. ( )

EXERCISE **4** Write Facts, Explanations, Examples, and Anecdotes

Work with a partner. Read each topic sentence and add *facts*, *explanations*, *examples*, **and** *anecdotes* **as support.**

1. Tokyo DisneySea is a very popular tourist destination.

How do I know?

Fact:

Every year, millions of people go to Tokyo DisneySea with friends and family.

Explanation:

Since the only DisneySea is in Japan, many people travel there from all over the world to see their favorite characters and ride the unique attractions.

How can I show this?

Example:

For example, Tower of Terror is so popular that visitors will wait for hours to ride it.

Anecdote:

My best friend pays for an annual pass and goes at least four times a year.

2. Kyoto is most beautiful in the autumn.

How do I know?

Fact:

_____

_____

Explanation:

_____

_____

How can I show this?
Example:

_____

_____

Anecdote:

_____

_____

3. Japanese food is healthy.

How do I know?
Fact:

_____

_____

Explanation:

_____

_____

How can I show this?
Example:

_____

_____

Anecdote:

_____

_____

OPPOSING OPINIONS

Focus on STRUCTURE Counter-arguments and Refutations

The **body sentences** provide major and minor support and explain why the reader should agree with the opinion stated in the topic sentence.

One important feature of the body sentences is the inclusion of a **counter-argument** and a **refutation**. The counter-argument expresses an opposing view to the writer's opinion.

To set up a counter-argument, you can use the simple phrase

> Some people may say that…

and then introduce the counter-argument.

Following the counter-argument, you will use a comma followed by *however* and then state your refutation. Your refutation can be one or more sentences. The point of the refutation is to convince your reader that the counter-argument is wrong.

Topic sentence	The climate in the desert varies a lot.
Counter-argument	**Some people may say that the desert is always hot,**

however, it can often be very cold. In many areas, it even snows.

EXERCISE 5 Refute Counter-arguments

Work with a partner. Read the counter-arguments below. Then write a refutation.

1. Some people may say that Tokyo is the best place in Japan to live,
<u>however, living in a smaller city is much more peaceful. There is far less stress.</u>

2. Some people may say that summer is better than winter,

_____

_____

3. Some people may say that college life is easier than life in high school,

_____

_____

4. Some people may say that they do not need to study a foreign language in school,

_____

_____

5. Some people may say that online classes are more convenient,

_____

_____

OPINIONS NOT PREFERENCES

Focus on MECHANICS Expressing Opinions not Preferences

Opinion paragraphs do not necessarily tell the reader what the writer prefers or likes. Even though it is your opinion, the paragraph should be written for people in general. In other words, it is not about you. It is about the reasons why your opinion is correct, and why the reader should agree. Consider these questions.

> Is social media good or bad for society (for everyone)?
> What is the best way to study (for people in general)?

You may like social media, and you may also have a way of studying that works for you. However, when you want to convince your reader that your opinion is correct, you must show that your opinion applies to everyone and is not just your preference.

While it is okay to give personal examples, a common problem is writing an opinion paragraph only from the perspective of the writer rather than for people in general.

EXERCISE 6 Discuss Your Opinions

Work with a partner. Read each of the questions and discuss your opinions. To get more ideas, it can be helpful to ask _why_? As you discuss your ideas with your partner, write down any ideas that may help you support your opinion.

1. Do you think college education should be free?

2. Is learning a foreign language important?

3. Do you think school uniforms should be mandatory?

EXERCISE 7 Let's Write

Choose one of the topics above and begin writing the first draft of an opinion paragraph. Start with your topic sentence, such as, *I think college education should be free, or I do not think learning a foreign language is important.* Then explain why you think so. Use the model paragraph and the lessons in this unit to help you.

✔ **Vocabulary** **Check the words you know, and review the words you do not.**

- ☐ Opinion
- ☐ Fact
- ☐ Explanation (review)
- ☐ Example (review)
- ☐ Anecdote (review)

- ☐ Reason
- ☐ Counter-argument
- ☐ Refutation

THE OPINION PARAGRAPH

"The pen is mightier than the sword!" —Edward Bulwer-Lytton

When you provide support for your opinions, you should organize your ideas in a way that seems reasonable to the reader. Just as process and narrative paragraphs use chronological order, and description paragraphs use spatial order, opinion paragraphs use **logical order** to organize and present the major supporting sentences. While there are many ways to create logical order in your writing, one of the simplest ways to present your supporting ideas is by **order of importance**. This means your last idea will provide the strongest support for your opinion.

EXERCISE **1** Read a Model Paragraph

Read the model paragraph. Then work with a partner to answer the questions below.

Cats not Dogs

When it comes to pets, there are three reasons why cats are far better than dogs. First, cats are quiet. They do not bark or make a big fuss around strangers or passing cars. They move quietly throughout the house or neighborhood and do not trouble anyone with loud noises. Second, cats keep themselves clean. Cats are always licking themselves and avoiding getting dirty. For instance, my cat will sit for long periods of time in the sun and licks herself. She takes incredible care and pride in staying clean. Dogs, on the other hand, like to play in the dirt, and their owners need to give them baths from time to time. Finally, and perhaps most importantly, cats are independent. Cats can stay home alone for long periods of time, and they are perfectly happy. They can get along all by themselves and do not need a lot of extra attention or care, like dogs do. For example, you do not need to take a cat on a walk every day like you do a dog. Some people claim that cats want to spend time with their owners in the same way dogs do. However, they are usually fine by themselves as long as they have enough food. To sum up, cats are better pets than dogs because they are quiet, clean, and independent. So, if you are thinking of getting a pet, get a cat. You will not regret it.

1. What is the topic sentence?

2. What is the writer's opinion?

3. How many reasons does the writer give to support his/her opinion?

4. What are the reasons?

5. What is the concluding sentence?

6. What is the purpose of the final sentence in the paragraph?

LOGICAL ORDERING

Focus on COHERENCE Order of Importance

As stated at the beginning of this unit, expressing your opinion will be more effective if you organize your ideas using logical ordering.

One way to achieve logical order in opinion paragraphs is to organize your supporting sentences by **order of importance**. This means that if you have one major supporting idea that you think is the strongest, you should put this as your final point and signal that support with a phrase such as:

Finally, and most importantly…
Lastly, the most important reason is…

Using order of importance for logical ordering will leave your reader with an impression that your opinion is a strong one, and they will be more likely to agree.

EXERCISE 2 Identify Logical Ordering

Work alone. Return to the model paragraph on page 94. Complete the exercises below. Then check your answers with a partner.

1. Draw a box around each of the major supporting sentences.
2. Circle the topic and underline the controlling idea.
3. Which major supporting sentence does the writer feel is most important?
4. Double underline the signal phrase the writer uses to highlight the most important major supporting sentence.

EXERCISE 3 Edit Your Draft

Work alone. Read your current opinion paragraph draft. Is there any major supporting sentence that is stronger than the others? If so, rearrange the order of your major and minor supporting sentences according to the order of importance. Then share your paragraph with a partner by reading it aloud.

IRRELEVANT SENTENCES

Focus on UNITY Staying Focused on the Topic

A common problem with supporting sentences is including information that does not support the main point of a passage. These **irrelevant sentences** may feel like you are giving examples or explanations, but in reality they make the writing unfocused and distract the reader. Read the example below.

(I) Cats are independent. (II) If you leave a little food and water for your cat, it will be okay all by itself. (III) My cat likes to eat canned food. (IV) Cats can stay home alone for long periods of time.

As we can see, sentence (III) does not belong in the passage. It does not add support to the main point of the passage that cats are *independent*. It is distracting and unfocused.

To identify irrelevant sentences in your writing, you must ask yourself three guiding questions:

1. Does each sentence support the main point of the passage?
2. Does each sentence relate the topic sentence of the paragraph?
3. Are there any sentences that are distracting or unfocused?

EXERCISE 4   Identify Irrelevant Sentences

Work with a partner. Take turns reading the excerpts. Then identify the irrelevant sentences. Discuss with your partner why you think this sentence is irrelevant.

1. (I) The Ryukyu Islands are a chain of islands that stretch from Kyushu to Taiwan. (II) There are over 100 islands in total. (III) The largest island is Okinawa. (IV) I went to Okinawa last year with my family. (V) The climate of the Ryukyu islands ranges from subtropical to tropical rainforest.

   Which sentence is irrelevant?   I   II   III   (IV)   V
   Why is it irrelevant?

   This paragraph is about the Ryukyu Islands, not about a family trip.

2. (I) The average human body is made up of 45-75% water. (II) Water is refreshing on a hot day. (III) These averages vary according to both age and sex. (IV) Adult males are usually made up of around 60% water, while adult females are around 55%. (V) Infants, on the other hand, are made up of nearly 75% water!

   Which sentence is irrelevant?   I   II   III   IV   V
   Why is it irrelevant?

   _____

3. (I) The best way to make new friends is to join a club or team. (II) There are lots of clubs and teams to choose from. (III) Clubs and teams are made up of people with similar interests. (IV) This means you can find people who are more like you. (V) My friend is not like me, but he is funny, so we get along great.

   Which sentence is irrelevant?   I   II   III   IV   V
   Why is it irrelevant?

   _____

4. (I) Last year, I had a scary experience while staying at my grandmother's old house in the countryside. (II) I was alone in the house when I heard a strange scratching noise coming from inside the closet. (III) I was so scared, but I had to open the door to see what it was. (IV) I am scared of ghosts. (V) I opened the door, and a bird flew out!

Which sentence is irrelevant?   I   II   III   IV   V
Why is it irrelevant?

_____

EXERCISE 5 Edit Your Partner's Draft

Work with a partner. Exchange your current opinion paragraph draft. Look for irrelevant sentences and discuss them with your partner. Be sure you ask yourself the three guiding questions discussed in the Irrelevant Sentences section of this unit.

CONCLUDING A PARAGRAPH

Focus on STRUCTURE Leaving a Final Impression

As stated in previous units, the concluding sentence(s) signal the end of the paragraph, restate the topic sentence in different words, and sometimes summarize the major points.

Topic sentence
When it comes to pets, cats are far better than dogs.

Concluding sentence
To sum up, cats are better pets than dogs because they are quiet, clean, and independent.

In an opinion paragraph, the concluding sentences may also leave the reader with a final opinion on the topic or ask the reader to do something.

Concluding sentence
To sum up, cats are better pets than dogs because they are quiet, clean, and independent. So, if you are thinking of getting a pet, get a cat. You will not regret it.

EXERCISE 6 Let's Write

Write the final draft of an opinion paragraph. Include all that you have learned in Units 11 and 12. Use the checklist below for help.

✓ Checklist

- [ ] My topic sentence states my opinion.
- [ ] My topic sentence includes a predictor. *(Optional)*
- [ ] My major supporting sentences are clear.
- [ ] I used facts for my minor supporting sentences.
- [ ] I used explanations for my minor supporting sentences.
- [ ] I used examples for my minor supporting sentences.
- [ ] I used anecdotes for my minor supporting sentences.
- [ ] I included one counter-argument and refutation.
- [ ] My paragraph is about my opinion not (necessarily) about my preference.
- [ ] I used order of importance to organize my major supporting sentences.
- [ ] I edited for irrelevant sentences.
- [ ] My paragraph has a concluding sentence.
- [ ] My paragraph is formatted correctly.

APPENDICES

Capitalization: What to Capitalize

1. The first letter in every sentence: **She** really loved the room.
2. The pronoun I: **I** love music.
3. Names of people: I talked to **Sara** yesterday.
4. The names of companies: I bought my earbuds from **Amazon**.
5. Days: The party is next **Saturday**.
6. Months: My birthday is **March** 15.
7. Holidays: Do you celebrate **Christmas**?
8. Nationalities: She is **French**.
9. Languages: He can speak **Spanish**.
10. Countries: They visited **Mexico** last summer.
11. Cities: Jun studied history at a university in **London**.
12. Continents: I have never been to **Europe**.

PRACTICE

1. **Read number 8 and 9 above. Work with a partner. List all the countries and nationalities you can think of.**

2. **Write an original sentence using each of the different noun types above. Capitalize correctly.**

   Example I spent **Christmas** in **South Africa** with my friend **Isabel**.

Coordinating Conjunctions: Making Compound Sentences

There are several coordinating conjunctions you can use to make compound sentences. You can remember them by the phrase *FAN BOYS. (for, and, nor, but, or, yet, so).*

Coordinating Conjunctions	Meaning/use	Example
For	To add a reason	She was not allowed to come, for she was not a member.
And	To add a similar, equal reason	I love movies, and I also love music.
Nor	To add a negative, equal reason	We could not see the sunset, nor could we go to the beach.
But	To add an opposite idea	Alison arrived on time, but the event was canceled.
Or	To add an alternative possibility	We will have a test tomorrow, or we will have it next week.
Yet	To add an unexpected result	He lies, yet she still believes him.
So	To add an expected result	It will rain today, so take an umbrella.

PRACTICE

1. **Work alone. After reading each of the example sentences. Write original sentences by changing the examples slightly.**

2. **Work with a partner. Read your sentences to your partner. Your partner will listen and write down what you read. Then switch. After finishing, compare what you have written with your partner's original sentences. Be sure to capitalize and punctuate correctly.**

Unit 8

Page 65

Adjective Order

Determiner	Number	Opinion	Size	Shape	Age	Color	Origin	Material	Purpose	Noun
A		beautiful	little			green				gem
					old		Italian	cotton	sports	T-shirts
That	Three				new					car
The	five	amazing	small	round		black	French	wooden		boxes
This						purple			sleeping	bag

Essential Writing 1
—From Sentence to Paragraph—

エッセンシャル・ライティング 1
——センテンスからパラグラフへ——

2023 年 1 月 20 日　初版第 1 刷発行
2023 年 2 月 20 日　初版第 2 刷発行

著　者　　Jethro Kenney

発行者　　**福 岡 正 人**
発行所　　株式会社　**金 星 堂**
（〒 101-0051）東京都千代田区神田神保町 3-21
Tel. (03) 3263-3828 (営業部)
(03) 3263-3997 (編集部)
Fax (03) 3263-0716
https://www.kinsei-do.co.jp

編集担当　今門貴浩　　　　　　　　　Printed in Japan
印刷所・製本所／倉敷印刷株式会社

ISBN978-4-7647-4180-5　C1082